MW01361783

Greetings
FROM
ALBANY
GEORGIA
The World's Greatest Paper Shell Pecan Center

Greetings
FROM
ALBANY
GEORGIA
The World's Greatest Paper Shell Pecan Center

Greetings
FROM
ALBANY
GEORGIA
The World's Greatest Paper Shell Pecan Center

Greetings
FROM
ALBANY
GEORGIA
The World's Greatest Paper Shell Pecan Center

Greetings
FROM
ALBANY
GEORGIA
The World's Greatest Paper Shell Pecan Center

Greetings
FROM
ALBANY
GEORGIA
The World's Greatest Paper Shell Pecan Center

Greetings
FROM
ALBANY
GEORGIA
The World's Greatest Paper Shell Pecan Center

Greetings
FROM
ALBANY
GEORGIA
The World's Greatest Paper Shell Pecan Center

Greetings
FROM
ALBANY
GEORGIA
The World's Greatest Paper Shell Pecan Center

Greetings
FROM
ALBANY
GEORGIA
The World's Greatest Paper Shell Pecan Center

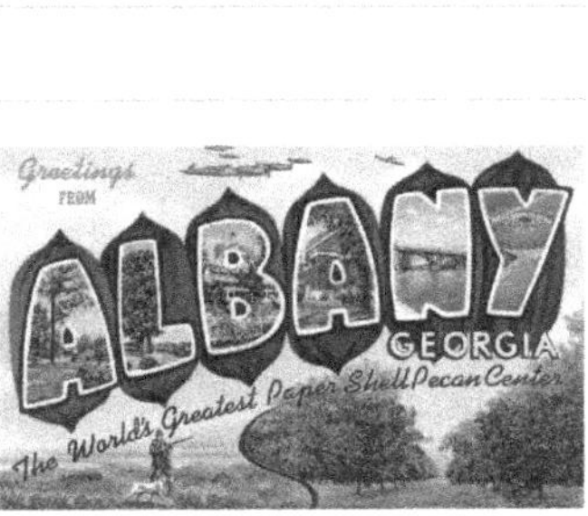
Greetings
FROM
ALBANY
GEORGIA
The World's Greatest Paper Shell Pecan Center

Greetings
FROM
ALBANY
GEORGIA
The World's Greatest Paper Shell Pecan Center

Greetings
FROM
ALBANY
GEORGIA
The World's Greatest Paper Shell Pecan Center

Greetings
FROM
ALBANY
GEORGIA
The World's Greatest Paper Shell Pecan Center

Greetings
FROM
ALBANY
GEORGIA
The World's Greatest Paper Shell Pecan Center

Greetings
FROM
ALBANY
GEORGIA
The World's Greatest Paper Shell Pecan Center

Greetings
FROM
ALBANY
GEORGIA
The World's Greatest Paper Shell Pecan Center

Greetings
FROM
ALBANY
GEORGIA
The World's Greatest Paper Shell Pecan Center

Greetings
FROM
ALBANY
GEORGIA
The World's Greatest Paper Shell Pecan Center

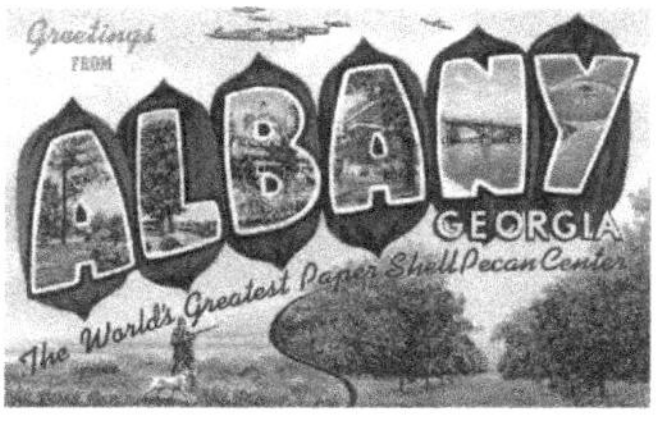
Greetings
FROM
ALBANY
GEORGIA
The World's Greatest Paper Shell Pecan Center

Greetings
FROM
ALBANY
GEORGIA
The World's Greatest Paper Shell Pecan Center

Greetings
FROM
ALBANY
GEORGIA
The World's Greatest Paper Shell Pecan Center

Greetings
FROM
ALBANY
GEORGIA
The World's Greatest Paper Shell Pecan Center

Greetings
FROM
ALBANY
GEORGIA
The World's Greatest Paper Shell Pecan Center

Greetings
FROM
ALBANY
GEORGIA
The World's Greatest Paper Shell Pecan Center

Greetings
FROM
ALBANY
GEORGIA
The World's Greatest Paper Shell Pecan Center

Greetings
FROM
ALBANY
GEORGIA
The World's Greatest Paper Shell Pecan Center

Greetings
FROM
ALBANY
GEORGIA
The World's Greatest Paper Shell Pecan Center

Greetings
FROM
ALBANY
GEORGIA
The World's Greatest Paper Shell Pecan Center

Greetings
FROM
ALBANY
GEORGIA
The World's Greatest Paper Shell Pecan Center

Greetings
FROM
ALBANY
GEORGIA
The World's Greatest Paper Shell Pecan Center

Greetings
FROM
ALBANY
GEORGIA
The World's Greatest Paper Shell Pecan Center

Greetings
FROM
ALBANY
GEORGIA
The World's Greatest Paper Shell Pecan Center

Greetings
FROM
ALBANY
GEORGIA
The World's Greatest Paper Shell Pecan Center

Greetings
FROM
ALBANY
GEORGIA
The World's Greatest Paper Shell Pecan Center

Greetings
FROM
ALBANY
GEORGIA
The World's Greatest Paper Shell Pecan Center

Greetings
FROM
ALBANY
GEORGIA
The World's Greatest Paper Shell Pecan Center

Greetings
FROM
ALBANY
GEORGIA
The World's Greatest Paper Shell Pecan Center

Greetings
FROM
ALBANY
GEORGIA
The World's Greatest Paper Shell Pecan Center

Greetings
FROM
ALBANY
GEORGIA
The World's Greatest Paper Shell Pecan Center

Greetings
FROM
ALBANY
GEORGIA
The World's Greatest Paper Shell Pecan Center

Greetings
FROM
ALBANY
GEORGIA
The World's Greatest Paper Shell Pecan Center

Greetings
FROM
ALBANY
GEORGIA
The World's Greatest Paper Shell Pecan Center

Greetings
FROM
ALBANY
GEORGIA
The World's Greatest Paper Shell Pecan Center

Greetings
FROM
ALBANY
GEORGIA
The World's Greatest Paper Shell Pecan Center

Greetings
FROM
ALBANY
GEORGIA
The World's Greatest Paper Shell Pecan Center

Greetings
FROM
ALBANY
GEORGIA
The World's Greatest Paper Shell Pecan Center

Greetings
FROM
ALBANY
GEORGIA
The World's Greatest Paper Shell Pecan Center

Greetings
FROM
ALBANY
GEORGIA
The World's Greatest Paper Shell Pecan Center

Greetings
FROM
ALBANY
GEORGIA
The World's Greatest Paper Shell Pecan Center

Greetings
FROM
ALBANY
GEORGIA
The World's Greatest Paper Shell Pecan Center

Greetings
FROM
ALBANY
GEORGIA
The World's Greatest Paper Shell Pecan Center

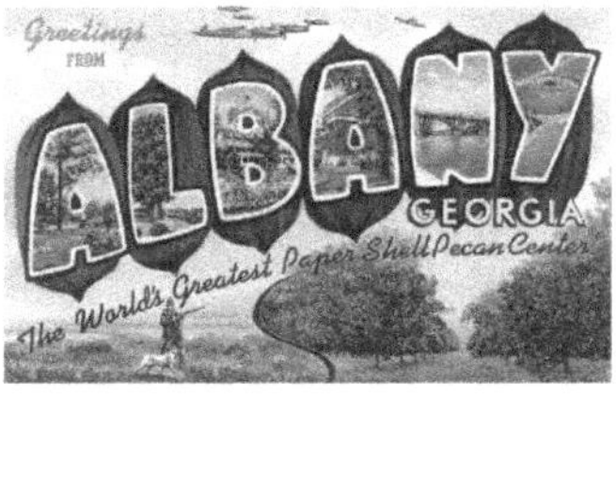
Greetings
FROM
ALBANY
GEORGIA
The World's Greatest Paper Shell Pecan Center

Greetings
FROM
ALBANY
GEORGIA
The World's Greatest Paper Shell Pecan Center

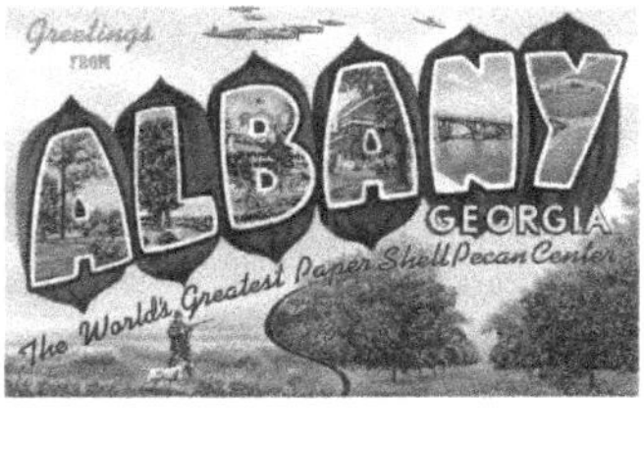
Greetings
FROM
ALBANY
GEORGIA
The World's Greatest Paper Shell Pecan Center

Greetings
FROM
ALBANY
GEORGIA
The World's Greatest Paper Shell Pecan Center

Greetings
FROM
ALBANY
GEORGIA
The World's Greatest Paper Shell Pecan Center

Greetings
FROM
ALBANY
GEORGIA
The World's Greatest Paper Shell Pecan Center

Greetings
FROM
ALBANY
GEORGIA
The World's Greatest Paper Shell Pecan Center

Greetings
FROM
ALBANY
GEORGIA
The World's Greatest Paper Shell Pecan Center

Greetings
FROM
ALBANY
GEORGIA
The World's Greatest Paper Shell Pecan Center

Greetings
FROM
ALBANY
GEORGIA
The World's Greatest Paper Shell Pecan Center

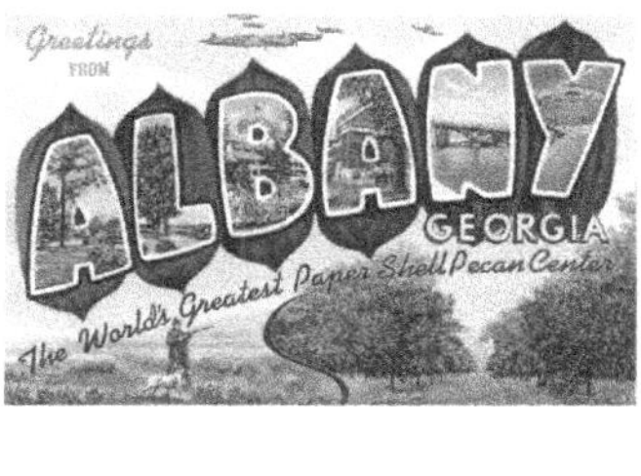
Greetings
FROM
ALBANY
GEORGIA
The World's Greatest Paper Shell Pecan Center

Greetings
FROM
ALBANY
GEORGIA
The World's Greatest Paper Shell Pecan Center

Greetings
FROM
ALBANY
GEORGIA
The World's Greatest Paper Shell Pecan Center

Greetings
FROM
ALBANY
GEORGIA
The World's Greatest Paper Shell Pecan Center

Greetings
FROM
ALBANY
GEORGIA
The World's Greatest Paper Shell Pecan Center

Greetings
FROM
ALBANY
GEORGIA
The World's Greatest Paper Shell Pecan Center

Greetings
FROM
ALBANY
GEORGIA
The World's Greatest Paper Shell Pecan Center

Greetings
FROM
ALBANY
GEORGIA
The World's Greatest Paper Shell Pecan Center

Greetings
FROM
ALBANY
GEORGIA
The World's Greatest Paper Shell Pecan Center

Greetings
FROM
ALBANY
GEORGIA
The World's Greatest Paper Shell Pecan Center

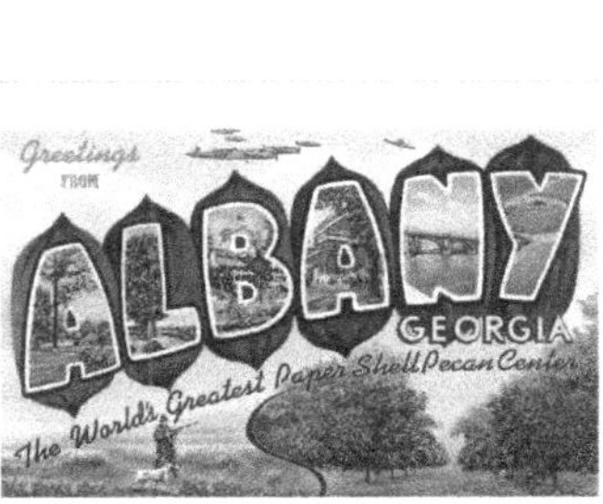
Greetings
FROM
ALBANY
GEORGIA
The World's Greatest Paper Shell Pecan Center

Greetings
FROM
ALBANY
GEORGIA
The World's Greatest Paper Shell Pecan Center

Greetings
FROM
ALBANY
GEORGIA
The World's Greatest Paper Shell Pecan Center

Printed in the USA
CPSIA information can be obtained
at www.ICGtesting.com
LVHW091733100524
779586LV00003B/133

9 798385 411733